KATIE COURIC
Groundbreaking TV Journalist

❝ *There are many people who will try to stand in your way. ... Learning this early on helped me believe in myself, even when [others] did not.* **❞** — Katie Couric

Life Portraits

KATIE COURIC
Groundbreaking TV Journalist

By Rachel Koestler-Grack

Gareth Stevens
Publishing

Please visit our web site at **www.garethstevens.com.**
For a free catalog describing Gareth Stevens Publishing's list of high-quality books,
call 1-800-542-2595 (USA) or 1-800-387-3178 (Canada).
Gareth Stevens Publishing's fax: 1-877-542-2596

Library of Congress Cataloging-in-Publication Data
Koestler-Grack, Rachel.
   Katie Couric, groundbreaking TV journalist / by Rachel Koestler-Grack.
      p. cm. — (Life portraits)
   Includes bibliographical references and index.
   ISBN–10: 1-4339-0056-4   ISBN–13: 978-1-4339-0056-3 (lib. bdg.)
   1. Couric, Katie, 1957- 2. Television personalities—United States—Biography.
3. Television news anchors—United States—Biography. I. Title.
PN1992.4.C68K64   2008
791.4502'8092—dc22
[B]   2008035781

This edition first published in 2009 by
Gareth Stevens Publishing
A Weekly Reader® Company
1 Reader's Digest Rd.
Pleasantville, NY 10570-7000 USA

Copyright © 2009 by Gareth Stevens, Inc.

Executive Managing Editor: Lisa M. Herrington
Creative Director: Lisa Donovan
Cover Designer: Keith Plechaty
Interior Designers: Yin Ling Wong and Keith Plechaty
Publisher: Keith Garton

Produced by Spooky Cheetah Press
www.spookycheetah.com
Editor: Stephanie Fitzgerald
Designer: Kimberly Shake
Cartographer: XNR Productions, Inc.
Proofreader: Jessica Cohn
Photo Researcher: Amy Dunleavy
Indexer: Madge Walls, All Sky Indexing

Printed in the United States of America

1 2 3 4 5 6 7 8 9 12 11 10 09 08

TABLE OF CONTENTS

In 1992, First Lady Barbara Bush gave Katie a tour of the White House. When it was over, Katie conducted a tough, on-the-spot interview with President George H. W. Bush.

CHAPTER ONE

BREAKING NEW GROUND

I N OCTOBER 1992, *TODAY* SHOW CO-ANCHOR KATIE Couric was given a tour of the White House by First Lady Barbara Bush. At the time, President George H. W. Bush was running for reelection against Democrat Bill Clinton.

As they walked from room to room, Mrs. Bush pointed out the interesting features of the house and entertained Katie with amusing stories about her experiences as first lady. When the tour ended, Katie decided to turn her attention to more serious matters. She was asking Mrs. Bush about her husband's campaign when, suddenly, the president walked into the room. He was surrounded by Secret Service agents.

Katie started peppering the president with difficult questions. Bush told Katie he was just passing through. He was not there to be interviewed. Katie didn't give up, though. She managed to pull Bush into a 20-minute, on-the-spot interview.

A reporter would ordinarily spend days preparing for such an important interview. He or she would conduct exhaustive research and write and rewrite questions until they were perfect. On this day, however, Katie had to think on her feet. She managed to keep the president talking with a mixture of small talk and tough questions on the upcoming election.

Jeff Zucker, the producer of the *Today* show, was watching from the studio control room. He could hardly believe what he was seeing. "It was one of the most remarkable moments of broadcast journalism I've ever seen," he recalled.

> **"It was one of the most remarkable moments of broadcast journalism I've ever seen."**
>
> – TODAY SHOW PRODUCER JEFF ZUCKER

CHANGING THE FACE OF TV NEWS

Katie is famous for catching people off guard during interviews. Her persistence and determination to hook and handle difficult interviews have catapulted her to celebrity status. From 1991 to 2006, she was a popular co-host of the NBC morning program the *Today* show. With her bubbly personality and no-holds-barred interviewing style, Katie quickly became one of the most popular personalities in morning TV.

On September 5, 2006, Katie became the first female solo anchor of the *CBS Evening News*. She is also the managing editor of the *CBS Evening News*, a *60 Minutes* correspondent, and an anchor of CBS News specials. Early on, Katie struggled to be taken seriously in her career. People called her "cute" and "perky," but Katie has shown that she means business.

THE COURIC EFFECT

Throughout her career, Katie has interviewed an extraordinary and diverse collection of newsmakers—from presidents and foreign leaders to celebrities and cultural icons. She began her career as a desk assistant at ABC News in Washington and worked her way into becoming a cultural icon herself.

Women in Broadcasting

Years ago, women had a hard time even getting a chance to do news on the radio. In those early days, most of the voices on the air were male. The small number of women who got radio jobs were almost always on entertainment broadcasts or on programs targeted at homemakers. Gradually, though, more and more women began taking over jobs in broadcast news, both on the radio and TV.

Over the years, women in broadcasting have faced many obstacles. Like Katie, they often faced discrimination because of their voices. Network executives believed women did not sound authoritative enough, and therefore should not deliver the news. That idea has been largely discredited, but women still face other issues of discrimination. For example, women have to worry about growing old in front of a TV audience. Men usually don't. A man with gray hair is often considered distinguished. The same attitude does not typically apply to women.

Katie has used her fame to promote cancer awareness and to encourage routine cancer screenings. It is a cause that is close to Katie's heart. Her husband, Jay Monahan, died from colon cancer in 1998. Her sister Emily died of pancreatic cancer in 2001. Cancer screenings can help prevent the disease and catch it in the early stages, which offers more hope for treatment. Katie had an on-air colonoscopy as a way of encouraging people to get tested. Some viewers followed her lead and were able to catch their cancer in its early stages. Many credit Katie for saving their lives. Her fearlessness in going through the invasive procedure—and speaking openly about it—had an enormous impact. Colon-

Some people have tried to dismiss Katie's credentials as a serious news journalist. But she has proven herself time and again, often in dangerous situations, such as a visit to war-torn Iraq.

cancer screenings rose 20 percent nationwide. Researchers credit this dramatic increase to what they call "the Couric Effect."

Katie's winning personality and warm smile have drawn viewers from all walks of life. Until she left *Today* in May 2006, millions of people across America started their mornings with a cup of coffee and Katie Couric. After she moved to CBS, Americans ended their day with her instead. Through it all, Katie continues to be an inspiration for anyone fighting the odds. ❖

When Katie was growing up, people called her "Smiley." From the time she was a kid, Katie's bubbly, outgoing personality served her well.

CHAPTER TWO

The Little Girl With the Big Smile

O N January 7, 1957, John Martin Couric and his wife Elinor welcomed their fourth child into the world. They named her Katherine Anne and called her Katie for short. Katie's siblings, Emily, Clara (Kiki), and Johnny, were thrilled to have a new baby in the house.

Katie was raised in Arlington, Virginia, not far from Washington, D.C. There, little Katie entertained her first audience. "She was a cutup," Emily remembered. "Even when she was an infant, we'd put her in her plastic seat and then all sit around and watch her."

Katie resembled her mother from the time she was a little girl. She had sparkling eyes and what Katie later called "chipmunk cheeks." Katie's mother had another influence on her daughter, too. Elinor, an outspoken feminist, inspired Katie to be strong, independent, and ambitious. When she was just a young girl,

Katie's mother instilled in her the belief that being a woman was neither an excuse for failure nor a barrier for success. Elinor taught her daughters that nothing was beyond their reach. She told them to live in the spotlight, not in the shadows. "Let them know you're here!" she said, "Don't just sit back in the crowd. Get out there and make your presence known."

AN IMPORTANT LESSON

Ever since Katie was a little girl, people called her "Smiley." A broad, gummy, slightly lopsided smile was almost constantly spread across her face. When Katie was in eighth grade, she learned a valuable lesson about how to use her smile to her advantage. On a crisp fall morning, she arrived at the door of Mrs. Barton's fourth-grade class. As hall monitor at Jamestown Elementary School, Katie had to deliver a message to the younger students. Everyone was standing up when Katie walked into the room. The class was still reciting the Pledge of Allegiance. As Katie entered the room, the entire class turned to see who had disturbed them. Katie flashed an embarrassed smile. Instead of smiling back, the students just stared at her. Mrs. Barton looked at Katie with annoyance and said, "Katie, you smile too much." The little girl felt her face grow red hot in humiliation.

> **"Let them know you're here! Don't just sit back in the crowd. Get out there and make your presence known."**
>
> – ELINOR COURIC

All day long, Katie could not shake her feelings of embarrassment. That evening, she told her father about what happened.

Katie (middle) has a close relationship with her mother (left) and father (right). For years, she called her parents after each Today *show episode to get her dad's feedback.*

"I can't help the way I smile," said Katie. "What should I do?" John was quick to respond to his daughter's problem. "Just use her words to your advantage," he said. He explained that it isn't just words that hurt people but also the way they react to them. Katie had the power to make Mrs. Barton's words meaningless. She just had to choose not to let them bother her.

> ### "Katie, you smile too much."
>
> – MRS. BARTON, TEACHER

For several days, Katie thought about what her father had said. Before she knew it, she had a chance to put his advice into practice. At the time, she was running for president of the Jamestown student council. As she was writing her campaign speech, her father suggested she use a spunky opening. Katie took his advice, writing:

> *Hello, my name is Katie Couric. People wonder why I am always smiling. It's because I am happy. Happy to go to such a wonderful school. Yes, Jamestown is a wonderful school and I'd like to keep it that way.*

Katie won the election by 13 votes. From that day on, she decided not to take other people's negative comments to heart. She realized that sometimes people would try to stand in her way. She learned that people act this way because of their own problems and shortcomings, not hers. She later remarked:

> *There are many people who will try to stand in your way, even cut you off at the knees for whatever reason, but it is often more about them than about you. Learning this early on helped me believe in myself, even when some of those around me did not.*

HIGH SCHOOL DAYS

Growing up, Katie was constantly clamoring for praise from her parents. She struggled to keep from being eclipsed by her older sisters. She quickly realized she could never hope to match Emily or Kiki—who were so much older—in knowledge or maturity. However, she managed to attract attention with her clever, playful behavior. Katie's outgoing personality shined through no matter where she went, but she was never obnoxious. "She was

Katie got into the spirit of things at her high school's Sadie Hawkins dance. For this event, the girls ask the boys to the dance, not the other way around.

very much the entertainer as a kid," one family friend recalled. Well-behaved and courteous, Katie always seemed to be smiling and laughing.

Education was very important to Katie's parents. From a young age, the Couric children were encouraged to expand their knowledge. Every evening at the dinner table, they were expected to present a new word they had learned that day. For the most part, Emily and Kiki dominated the discussion. They excelled

Giving of Herself

Education wasn't the only thing that was important to the Courics. The kids were also encouraged to be charitable. After her freshman year, Katie took a summer job as a counselor for the Columbia Lighthouse for the Blind Day Camp. She was responsible for eight campers who were four or five years old. One day, the counselors took their campers on a field trip to the National Air and Space Museum in Washington, D.C. One of Katie's campers, Carolyn, was too afraid to ride the escalator. With patience and understanding, Katie reassured the frightened child that the moving stairs were safe. Eventually, she convinced Carolyn to give them a try. This incident taught Katie how to be a patient, sympathetic listener and how to put people at ease. These were gifts that would come in handy years later in her life as an interviewer.

in high school and were cheerleaders and student leaders. After they graduated, both girls attended Smith College, a top women's college in Northampton, Massachusetts.

In school, Katie followed in her sisters' footsteps—to a certain degree. Like Kiki and Emily, Katie was a cheerleader and student leader at Yorktown High School in Arlington. However, unlike her studious older sisters, Katie was more interested in boys than in her schoolwork.

REFOCUSED FOR SUCCESS

For most of her school years, Katie's report cards were hardly impressive. "I was a real clown who goofed off a lot," she later admitted. She realized that if she wanted to get into a good college, she would have to start taking her schoolwork seriously. When she was a junior, she finally started buckling down and studying. That year, she got straight As. Still, the grades from her early high-school years held her back. Like her sisters, Katie applied to Smith College, but she was not accepted. Instead, she decided to go to the University of Virginia (UVa), one of the best colleges in the state. Katie graduated from Yorktown High School in the spring of 1975. That fall, she set out for UVa in Charlottesville.

> **"I was a real clown who goofed off a lot."**
>
> – KATIE COURIC

Katie joined the cheerleading team at Yorktown High School. When she was younger, Katie used to say the worst thing that ever happened to her was not making captain of the squad.

Katie's Alma Mater

Katie often talks about her experiences at the University of Virginia. She is proud of her alma mater—the university from which she graduated. UVa ranks as one of the best public universities in America. The campus sits on 1,800

acres in the foothills of the Blue Ridge Mountains, about 120 miles (193 kilometers) south of Washington, D.C. Its founder, Thomas Jefferson, called it an academic village and designed its main rotunda building after the Parthenon in Athens. First opened in 1825, the school did not allow female students until 1970—just five years before Katie enrolled.

Katie's bubbly, friendly personality helped her slip effortlessly into college life. She became an associate editor of *The Cavalier Daily*, the campus newspaper, and joined the elite Delta Delta Delta sorority. Even though Katie was part of a sorority, she had friends from all different social circles.

At UVa, Katie followed in her father's footsteps. After serving in World War II, John became a journalist. The journalism courses Katie took helped her sculpt a series of articles for the *Cavalier* titled "Professor Profiles." They were flattering stories about the most powerful faculty members. Before long, Katie knew practically

> **"You just never know who you are going to need."**
>
> — KATIE COURIC

every member of the faculty and the administration. A classmate asked her why she was so friendly with the old professors. "You just never know who you are going to need," Katie replied.

During the summers, Katie interned at radio stations. There, she learned how to conduct interviews. With a little urging from her father, she chose broadcasting as her career. She was the only one in the family to follow her dad into the news business.

PURSUING HER DREAM

Katie planned each step of her college career with intense foresight. She believed in making connections that would help her succeed. Although she could be compassionate and kind, Katie never let her emotions get in the way of what she wanted—even if it meant muscling out a friend who was striving for the same goal she had. If she wanted something, she could be pretty tough. A classmate of hers later recalled:

Katie could be ruthless about getting where she wanted to go. She was very political about school, which I thought at the time was rather extraordinary. Most of the kids just tried to get good grades and have a decent time. With her, everything was a political calculation.

Throughout her college years, Katie weaved big dreams. Once, Katie confided to her boyfriend that her goal was to be the next Barbara Walters. At the time, Walters was co-anchoring ABC's *World News Tonight*. Katie wanted to become an anchor at a major network and have a show of her own. Anchoring a newscast is a prestigious job. The anchor delivers top news stories to the entire country. When Katie was in college, few women held

Barbara Walters

Barbara Walters is a famous American journalist, writer, and television personality. She has appeared regularly on morning and daytime television shows, first on *Today* and later on *The View*. In 1976, she became the first woman to co-anchor a network evening news program, ABC's *World News Tonight*. Barbara is well known for her years on the evening newsmagazine *20/20*, as well as many ABC News specials. She has interviewed everyone from numerous U.S. presidents and world leaders, such as Anwar Sadat, to pop culture icons, such as Tom Hanks. Barbara's habit of asking moving personal questions has made her famous for making her interview subjects cry. "Barbara's the queen," Katie once said. "I think once you build up a track record and you've interviewed so many world leaders, and so many people have entrusted their stories to you, that definitely works to [Barbara's] advantage. She never takes a breather. She's always in there."

In college, Katie had dreams of becoming a famous co-anchor like Barbara Walters (left).

these types of positions. Most women in television news covered the light stories, not the hard-hitting news. In 1979, Katie graduated from the University of Virginia with a bachelor's degree in English and a focus on American studies. She had dreams of being a television star. ❖

Katie wouldn't let anything stand in the way of her goal. It took hard work and a lot of grit, but she eventually achieved her dream of stardom.

CHAPTER THREE

BIG DREAMS

I N THE LATE 1970S, JOBS IN THE BROADCASTING field were hard for women to find. Katie was optimistic that she could get what she wanted out of life anyway. She was ambitious, confident, and fiercely competitive. Luckily, she also knew a few people in the business.

All of the major television networks—CBS, NBC, and ABC—had their main offices in New York City. However, each network also had a smaller office in Washington, D.C. Shortly after graduation, Katie walked into the office of the ABC News Washington bureau. Somehow she convinced the security guard to put her on the phone with the executive producer of *World News Tonight*. "Hi, Davy, you don't know me," Katie said, "but your twin brothers Steve and Eddie went to high school with my sister Kiki, and I live down the street from your cousin Julie." Then she asked if she could come up to his office.

Thanks to Kiki—and a bit of nerve—Katie got her foot in the door. She landed a job as a desk assistant, which is where most major news anchors get their start. Her job consisted mainly of brewing coffee, answering phones, and running out to fetch the occasional sandwich. On her first day of work, White House correspondent Sam Donaldson invited Katie to join him for a White House briefing. Donaldson later recalled:

> She clearly was one of those desk assistants who had it. I didn't turn to someone and say, 'There is the star of tomorrow.' But I did turn to someone and say, 'Hey, she's cute.'

Over the following months, Katie became confident that TV journalism was right for her. Her stay at ABC did not last long, though. Less than a year after she started her job, the ABC News Washington bureau chief moved to Cable News Network (CNN). He decided to take a few staff members with him to the new CNN Washington bureau. Katie was one of them.

NEW OPPORTUNITIES, NEW CHALLENGES

Katie's move to CNN came with a promotion. She became an assignment editor. Katie handed out ideas to reporters and told them which stories needed to be covered each day. The promotion had its challenges. The biggest one was the attitude shared by the veteran journalists who had launched the network. Katie hoped to one day work her way up to news anchor. These tough newsmen had trouble taking her seriously, though. She certainly

While working as a correspondent, Katie attended many press briefings, like this one, at the White House.

had the brains and plenty of energy, but she did not fit the mold of CNN's female news anchors—beautiful blondes. Katie was cute, but in a girlish sort of way.

Katie also suffered from stage fright. The minute the camera started to roll her hands fluttered, her voice grew shaky, and she stumbled over her words. She also had a high-pitched, untrained voice. It did not match the serious tone the country's first 24-hour news network was trying to achieve. Despite her short-comings, Katie got a few opportunities to prove herself on air.

One morning, an anchor failed to show up for work. The producer running the show had 23-year-old Katie take his place.

All News All the Time

On Sunday, June 1, 1980, the Cable News Network (CNN) first appeared on televisions across the country. The network has 36 bureaus—10 in the United States and 26 internationally—more than 900 affiliated local stations, and several regional and foreign-language networks around the world. A companion network, Headline News (originally called CNN2), was launched on January 1, 1982. This network featured the first 24-hour news station. It introduced continuous 30-minute news broadcasts, paving the way for other networks to follow suit.

Reese Schonfeld, one of CNN's founders, got a call telling him that Katie was on the air. He turned on the TV and got his first impression of Katie, "white-faced and scared stiff, and looking all of fourteen." Schonfeld immediately called the producer and said, "I never want to see her on the air again."

> **"I never want to see her on the air again."**
>
> – REESE SCHONFELD, CNN CO-FOUNDER

Katie's hopes for a career as a broadcast reporter seemed dashed. In fact, she heard a rumor that the managing editor of CNN's Washington bureau was going to fire her. She ran to her friend, medical correspondent Jean Carper, in a panic. Carper immediately called Schonfeld in Atlanta. "Katie's in tears," she told him. "She's crying because Stuart Loory's about to fire her. I think it'd be a big loss to CNN if that should happen." Schonfeld had a great deal of respect for Carper's opinion. So, he found a new spot for Katie. She was given a job as a junior producer on an afternoon news and information show called *Take Two*. The program was modeled after the *Today* show. On Thanksgiving Day in 1980, Katie stuffed her clothes into a large suitcase. The next day, she drove 10 hours to her new job at CNN's headquarters in Atlanta. ❖

During her early days at CNN, Katie's future in broadcasting was hardly certain. Before long, though, she would rise to stardom on the Today *show.*

CHAPTER FOUR

GETTING SERIOUS

DON FARMER AND CHRIS CURLE, A POPULAR husband-and-wife team, co-anchored *Take Two*. They were thrilled to have Katie on board. Occasionally, they even let her go on air as part of their program. During this time, Katie also took voice lessons to improve her on-air tone quality. Her work paid off. Before long, she was offered a position as a full-time on-air correspondent for the show. As an on-air correspondent, Katie reported daily from various locations. In an attempt to make herself appear professional and mature, Katie used her full name—Katherine Couric—as her sign-off.

In April 1982, Katie got an incredible opportunity. CNN was allowed to broadcast live from Havana, Cuba. It was the first American network allowed to do so since the Cuban Revolution in 1959. Farmer and Curle took Katie along to produce the three-hour program. In Havana, Katie worked on the daily live feeds—no small feat in a foreign country. Katie spoke very little Spanish. At night, she sprawled out on the floor, surrounded by research books, trying to sift through the language and figure out a way to produce a smooth and sensational show. During the day, she did her best to direct the local technicians with her choppy Spanish. Luckily, the technicians took a liking to Katie. "She had them eating out of her hands," recalled Farmer. "She was her cute self, yet very tough."

Land of Secrets

For decades, Cuba has protected its isolation. Cuban dictator Fidel Castro had a tight grip on any information coming into the country and any news leaking out. In 1969, the Associated Press was kicked out of the country, and Castro shut Cuba's doors to American journalists. All that began to change in 1982 when Castro agreed to allow CNN into Cuba. Why Castro chose CNN over other networks was quite simple. He liked CNN boss Ted Turner. They were more than just business associates. They were pals and had even gone fishing together. Since CNN stepped into Cuba, other networks and reporters have also made their way into the secretive country. From time to time, a reporter runs a story that the Cuban government does not like. Although Castro is no longer in power, the consequence for publishing such a story is still deportation.

Katie covered the 1984 presidential election, in which President Ronald Reagan ran against a former vice president, Walter Mondale.

After returning from Cuba, Katie was made a political correspondent for *Take Two*. She went on the road doing profiles on candidates in the 1982 elections. Then, in 1984, she covered the presidential elections, in which Democratic candidate Walter Mondale ran against Republican Ronald Reagan. Katie's on-air performance was still not impressing her bosses. In the eyes of Burt Reinhardt, who by this time was running CNN, Katie did not look, act, or sound like a serious journalist. One day after the election, he told executive vice president of news gathering, Ed Turner, to take Katie off the air—permanently. "She makes things look frivolous," he said. "That's not CNN."

Katie was crushed. For the next several months, she brooded about her poor reviews. She even wondered whether she had what it took to become a news anchor, but she refused to give up on her dream. She knew she had things to work on, and the lack of support from her bosses made her more determined to succeed. It was time to get serious. "I stunk," she later admitted. "I had nobody on my way up saying, 'We're going to make you a star,' and I think that really helped me," she said. "It forced me to work."

> "I had nobody on my way up saying, 'We're going to make you a star,' and I think that really helped me. It forced me to work."
>
> – KATIE COURIC

REWORKING HER STYLE

Katie had amassed four years of experience in the television news business. She had worked behind the scenes and in front of the camera. However, Katie still battled one discouraging obstacle that was keeping her from realizing her dream. Nobody took her seriously. Katie's director and boyfriend, Guy Pepper, offered to help. He put together a video resume of her best work and sent it to news directors at several TV stations. Pepper also tutored Katie in television technique. She fine-tuned the way she pronounced words. She slowed down the rhythm of her speech and learned to control her body movements. She even changed the way she wore her hair and makeup. Even though she was nearly 29 years old, Katie looked much younger. She cut her hair short, hoping it would make her look more sophisticated.

Katie got tired of people calling her "cute." She even tried a shorter hairstyle, hoping it would make her look more mature.

Katie's hard work paid off. In the fall of 1984, she was called in for an interview at Miami's NBC affiliate station, WTVJ. The news director offered her a position as a TV reporter. As she headed down Interstate 95 toward Miami, Katie hoped her luck was about to change. Perhaps she would become a star at WTVJ Channel 6, Florida's leading television station.

NIGHT-BEAT REPORTER

Katie's decision to go to Miami was a smart one. In the mid-1980s, two main areas provided excellent exposure for talented young broadcasters. One area was Hartford, because many network executives owned homes in Connecticut. The other was Miami, because Florida was a popular vacation spot for many network executives.

At WTVJ, Katie worked as a night-beat reporter. That is someone who searches the nighttime streets for stories—often about crime. Katie's arrival in Miami could not have been timed better. The city seethed with violence and corruption. Not long after Katie started at WTVJ, the FBI announced that the Miami-Dade metropolitan area had topped Detroit, Michigan, as the most dangerous city in America. There is a saying in local TV news—if it bleeds, it leads—and Miami was a hotbed for bloody news. Al Bunch, the news director who hired Katie, remarked about what a great opportunity this was:

What a place for a young journalist to learn her craft, for Pete's sake. One day, a drug house would blow up. Another, one hundred people would drown off the coast of Florida trying to come to the U.S. illegally. Cigarette boats running drugs off the coast got busted. … Police officers were being arrested for murdering traffickers in cold blood and then stealing their drugs.

While working the night beat, Katie sometimes reported on two stories a day. Often, her reports revolved around drugs, crime, cops, and immigration. However, she covered other general interest topics, as well. On August 12, 1986, Katie delivered a special report on global warming. She tried to get the public thinking about greenhouse gases and holes in the ozone layer, claiming that people were "stepping on mother nature in the name of progress." Katie even questioned whether residents of Miami would be able to breathe the air and drink the water by the year 2000.

Later that month, Katie put together a story called "Street People" about the homeless. For the feature, she dressed up like a homeless person and begged for money, wiped car windshields, and even waded through the fountain of the Intercontinental Hotel to fish out pennies.

BREAKING OUT

At last, Katie was beginning to find her voice. She dropped the idea that a newswoman had to be serious, solemn, and cold. Instead, she started to relax and let her true self shine through. People began to take notice. "I had my eye on Katie," said Donald Brown, NBC's bureau chief in Miami. "She was a terrific general assignment reporter, gutsy and good. She had network correspondent written all over her." A television critic also commented on Katie's improvement. "She was developing star presence," he said.

Still, Katie's bosses continued to hold her back. Once, Katie received a tip that the FBI was in the thick of a blazing shoot-out in South Miami. This was the kind of story that could catapult a reporter into the spotlight. Covering a hard news segment could prove her talent and worthiness as a news anchor. Katie called the news desk and begged for the assignment. She could have been on the scene in just a few minutes. Instead, her boss sent a more experienced reporter who

> "I had my eye on Katie. She was a terrific general assignment reporter, gutsy and good. She had network correspondent written all over her."
>
> – DONALD BROWN, NBC BUREAU CHIEF IN MIAMI

Network executives questioned her style, but Katie's fun, down-to-earth personality made her a hit with television viewers.

was more than 40 minutes away. "[Katie] worked her butt off, but she couldn't get a break," said a fellow reporter named Lu Ann Cahn. "They always saw her as the cub reporter, because she was so cute and looked so young."

At that time, network producers still thought a female reporter should look sophisticated, mature, and serious. Katie's girlish look and bubbly style were a turnoff for most network bigwigs. They worried the ratings would suffer if they gave Katie a job as a hard-hitting TV journalist.

The lack of support from her bosses made Katie doubt her goals. Perhaps she really did lack the looks and finesse of a news anchor. Maybe she would have to settle for being a reporter. "I always thought of myself as the workhorse, street-reporter type," she later said. "And besides, my bosses never encouraged me." Once again, Katie was doubting whether she had chosen the right path. She was almost ready to give up on her dreams. Then a couple of big breaks arrived just in the nick of time. ❖

"[Katie] worked her butt off, but she couldn't get a break. They always saw her as the cub reporter, because she was so cute and looked so young."

– LU ANN CAHN, WHO WORKED WITH KATIE IN MIAMI

In 1991, Katie became the new co-host of the Today show, sharing the spotlight with Bryant Gumbel.

CHAPTER FIVE

KATIE'S BIG BREAK

N O ONE WAS GOING TO COME LOOKING FOR Katie to offer her a job. Even if there was a chance of that happening, she wasn't the type of person to wait around. Instead, Katie got an agent and put together a resume tape. Her agent sent the tape to Jim Van Messel, the news director for WRC-TV, NBC's affiliate in Washington, D.C. Van Messel turned it over to the general manager of the station, who liked what he saw. He thought Katie was one of the most natural and spontaneous people on television. WRC-TV was looking for someone to do live reports at 11:00 each night. Katie's ability to report any kind of story made her perfect for the position. By the beginning of 1987, the reporter was back in Washington.

Before long, Katie was doing features about ordinary people struggling to overcome adversity. She seemed to be the ideal reporter for these types of stories. Perhaps that was because she could really relate to the people. After all, she was going through her own struggles in an industry that seemed intent on holding her back. Katie's ability to show compassion on camera propelled her to a new level.

Katie believed she was ready to take the next step to the anchor's chair. However, her news director felt differently. Because she was used to live reporting, Van Messel thought Katie would have trouble reading the Teleprompter—the screen that news anchors read from to report the news. When Katie asked for a chance to anchor, Van Messel told her that she needed more experience. He suggested she start in a small city somewhere. "Like Casper, Wyoming," he said. He was trying to say that Katie should start out in some unknown place and work her way up from there. Of course, Katie had other ideas.

What Van Messel didn't know was that a new era in television news had already begun—one that was tailor-made for Katie Couric. The very things that had been holding her back— her average appearance, her lack of sophistication and style, her playful personality, and her fearlessness in front of powerful people—would prove to be her strengths. Meanwhile, Katie's personal life was about to undergo a major change, as well.

MEETING MISTER RIGHT

From the time she graduated college, Katie had placed her full attention on her career. She was more interested in landing a big story than finding the right man. In the back of her mind, Katie wondered whether she could have both a demanding job and a family. Then, in early 1989, all that changed. Katie went to a party in Falls Church, Virginia. There were lots of eligible bachelors there—most of them lawyers. As Katie approached a group of men, one of them asked what she did for a living. "I'm a reporter at WRC-TV," she replied. "What do you guys do?" Practically at the same time, they all answered, "We're lawyers." Katie thought lawyers were dull and arrogant. In typical Katie style, she let the men know exactly how she felt. She turned her head to the side and stuck a couple of fingers in her mouth pretending to gag herself. Seeing that Katie was unimpressed with his profession, one of the attorneys decided to make a joke. "I'm a painter," he said with a smile. The comment caught Katie's attention, and the two began talking. John Paul Monahan III was a litigator at a prestigious Washington, D.C., law firm.

Jay Monahan was Katie's "Mister Right." The couple married just a year after their first date.

Monahan, whose friends simply called him Jay, was tall, thin, dark-haired, and handsome. Katie decided she wanted to get to know him a little better. Because of her take-charge personality, Katie had no trouble asking Jay on a date. She invited him to have lunch with her.

Katie and Jay hit it off right away, even though they had very different backgrounds. Jay grew up in a large Irish Catholic family in Manhasset, New York. After high school, he attended Washington and Lee University in Lexington, Virginia. That's where both Confederate Generals Robert E. Lee and Stonewall Jackson are buried. Surrounded by Civil War history, Jay developed an interest in the era. Later, at Georgetown Law School, he became a Civil War reenactor—someone who dresses up in a Civil War uniform and participates in reenactments of battles.

Katie was more outgoing and sociable than Jay was. Yet they were both intelligent, quick-witted, well-rounded individuals who believed family was important. They both enjoyed politics, history, and debating current issues. In 1989, about a year after their first date, Katie and Jay were married.

THE TOUGHEST BEAT

In July 1989, NBC offered Katie a new job. The studios of WRC-TV and the Washington bureau of NBC News were in the same building. Tim Russert, NBC's new bureau chief, was looking for a number-two reporter—or backup reporter—to cover the Pentagon. In his mind, Katie stood out. The Pentagon is the toughest beat in Washington. Because officials at the Pentagon hold national military secrets, reporters have a difficult time

Journalist Tim Russert (second from left) gave Katie (fourth from left) her first big break, and they often worked together over the years. Russert died suddenly in 2008.

getting people to talk. Information is hard to come by. On this beat, a reporter needs trustworthy sources. Without them, Katie would have a hard time reporting stories. In fact, it would be difficult just to find the stories. Katie had just the right personality for that part of the job. She had no trouble finding sources who would give her the scoop on breaking news.

Katie had been at the Pentagon for about six months when the United States invaded Panama on December 20, 1989. America's mission was to replace military dictator General Manuel Noriega with a democratic president. NBC's chief Pentagon correspondent, Fred Francis, went to Panama to cover the invasion. As

Making Connections

Katie immediately proved that she could find sources at the Pentagon. As she left the building on her third day of work, Katie realized she didn't remember where she'd parked her car. As she stood in the huge parking lot, Katie noticed two women who worked at the Department of Defense leaving the building. She asked them to point her toward the press parking lot. They offered to show her. As they walked, the women began chatting. Katie's friendly personality quickly won the others over.

The next morning, Katie got a phone call from one of the women. The lady tipped her off that a United States Air Force captain had been arrested in Berlin. He was accused of spying for the Soviet Union. Katie's story about the espionage led the *Nightly News* that Friday. "That's a perfect example of what a good reporter is," a colleague commented, "a relationship with sources."

backup reporter, Katie took over the live telecasts from the Pentagon. Her intelligent coverage of the event helped establish her as a serious reporter. "I think covering the Pentagon elevated me in the eyes of a lot of people," Katie said. "You can't be an airhead and cover F-14s." NBC executives were impressed. One week later they asked her to cover the Saturday evening news.

Reporting the Saturday evening news was a big break for Katie. An even bigger one came in May 1990. Executives at NBC asked her to be a national correspondent for the *Today* show. As a correspondent, Katie covered news features from around the country. Three months later, though, she returned to the Pentagon full time. Iraq had invaded the small country of Kuwait, and on August 7, U.S. forces were sent to the Persian Gulf. Once again, Katie was covering military news. The situation in Kuwait soon led to another military conflict—the Persian Gulf War (1991).

Katie's Pentagon contacts came in handy on January 16, 1991—the day the war began. An official tipped her off, telling her that she should not go home at 3:00 in the afternoon when her shift normally ended. "And that's how we knew that the air war was going to begin that night," Fred Francis later explained. Thanks to this tip, NBC broke the story. Their news team was the first to report that the country was at war.

> "I think covering the Pentagon elevated me in the eyes of a lot of people. You can't be an airhead and cover F-14s."
>
> – KATIE COURIC

During the Gulf War, Katie worked as the Pentagon correspondent for the *Today* show. Each morning, she reported to the Pentagon at 5:30 and was on the air at 7:00. Television viewers from around the world became more familiar with Katie's friendly face and matter-of-fact reporting style.

At one point in the war, Katie got the chance to visit Saudi Arabia for three weeks. Her first overseas assignment was to

After the Gulf War, Katie was the first person to interview General Norman Schwarzkopf, leader of the U.S. forces.

interview people who lived in the country and listen to their stories about how the war was affecting them. While she was there, she also spent time with American troops stationed in the desert. "They helped me appreciate—for the first time in my life—that war is really about people ... whose lives are at risk," Katie told *Redbook* magazine months later. After a cease-fire was declared on February 28, 1991, Katie was the first person to interview General Norman Schwarzkopf, leader of the U.S. forces.

On April 4, 1991, less than a year after she was hired as the *Today* show national correspondent, NBC asked Katie to be the show's co-anchor. She would be sharing the job with

Bryant Gumbel. Becoming a news anchor is the pinnacle of a TV journalist's career. Anchors are the stars of the news business. At 34 years old, Katie had finally landed the job she had always dreamed of having. In a little more than 10 years, she had moved up from desk assistant to anchor of a major network. Even more would come out of her new role than Katie could have ever imagined. She was about to ring in a new era of morning news programs. Katie was the fresh new face of TV news, and she would remain so for more than a decade. ❖

Katie worked with Deborah Norville (left) before taking over for her as co-host of the Today *show.*

CHAPTER SIX

A SELF-MADE STAR

I N APRIL 1991, NBC EXECUTIVES ASKED KATIE TO co-anchor the *Today* show alongside Bryant Gumbel. If she accepted, she would be replacing Deborah Norville. Katie had one condition for accepting the position, however. She insisted that she be assigned as many serious interviews as Gumbel, her co-anchor.

Oftentimes, female anchors were asked to only report on light-hearted stories. Norville never covered serious news while on *Today*. For the most part, Gumbel ran the show. Katie did not want that to happen to her. "That was one of the important conditions of my taking this job—I wasn't going to do all the Martha Stewart segments or lead-ins," Katie told a reporter for *Entertainment Weekly* magazine. "I've been in television journalism for 11 years, and I didn't want to be this sidekick who sort of giggled and did the features."

Katie made her debut on *Today* on April 5, 1991. Everyone at NBC saw right away that she would become the star of the show. "Everybody knew we had seen the future and it was Katie," said one executive.

"Everybody knew we had seen the future and it was Katie."

– NBC EXECUTIVE

Katie was on the air for two hours every morning, from 7:00 to 9:00. She also had to put in a lot of preparation time both before and after the show. On *Today*, the anchors sit in a conversation area, similar to a living room, where guests often join them. Gumbel was known for his fine interviews and for asking difficult questions. Before each

Katie Makes the Cut

Katie took over for Deborah Norville as co-anchor of the *Today* show. Norville had replaced previous co-host Jane Pauley, but the audience never warmed to her. Ratings plummeted as loyal viewers started turning their channels to rival network ABC's *Good Morning America*. Then, in February 1991, Norville took a maternity leave. Katie stepped in as her temporary replacement. As soon as Katie appeared on the show, the ratings jumped. In the cutthroat world of TV news, networks choose personalities that bring in the biggest audience. Katie was bringing in ratings that Norville could not.

Katie turned out to be an incredible asset to the Today *show team, which included sportscaster Joe Garagiola (left) and Bryant Gumbel (center).*

show, he spent a lot of time reading books and magazine articles about the guests he would be interviewing. He prepared just as much for a lighthearted interview as he for did a serious one.

Katie had to be just as dedicated as Gumbel. At first, she struggled to fit into her new role. Chatting with guests in a more social setting was totally different than reporting on serious news stories. "It was all very new to me and tough at first and I would get very uptight," Katie explained. The television viewers did not seem to mind. They took an immediate liking to Katie. She had a way of putting both the guests and the viewers at ease. Perhaps it was her down-to-earth, no-nonsense interviewing techniques. Or maybe it was her trademark cheeky smile.

Many people described the *Today* show's new co-host as "perky." She never cared for the term. To her, the word seems sexist and patronizing. "Bob Costas (the sports journalist) is short and cute," Katie explained, "but I've never heard him called 'perky.'" Another word often used to describe Katie was "cute." She did not like this description either. For 12 years, Katie had worked very hard to develop an image as a professional journalist. Somehow, *perky* and *cute* did not fit that image. Although Katie didn't like the labels, these personality traits certainly helped her appeal to viewers. "I think people see me as someone they could have gone to high school with, or someone who works at the desk next to them," Katie told *The New York Times*. "I'm ridiculously normal."

> "I think people see me as someone they could have gone to high school with, or someone who works at the desk next to them. I'm ridiculously normal."
>
> – KATIE COURIC

PART OF THE FAMILY

Co-anchoring *Today* was a difficult job, which took up much of Katie's time. Her new job was not the only challenge in her life. Jay worked in Washington, D.C. Not long after Katie accepted the job at *Today*, she and Jay moved into a two-bedroom apartment in the Washington, D.C., suburb of McLean, Virginia.

Because the *Today* studio was in New York City, Katie would have to get an apartment there and live apart from Jay Monday through Friday. They got to see each other every weekend, but the separation was difficult. The fact that Katie and Jay were expecting their first child made it even harder to be apart.

Meanwhile, Katie was becoming a perfect fit on the *Today* show. At the time, producer Jeff Zucker said:

> *Katie's the most natural person I've ever seen in this role. She's terrific. This is so new to her and she's getting better every day. She doesn't even realize how good she is.*

As the months passed, Katie's popularity continued to rise. So did the show's ratings. Before long, the *Today* show passed its biggest competitor, ABC's *Good Morning America,* in the

Katie became close friends with Today *show producer Jeff Zucker (right). He believed that Katie's down-to-earth personality was the future of morning television.*

Nielson ratings. "The hard part is finding a flaw," wrote television critic Tom Shales. "She's the everything gal. She's an apple a day. She's real, she's natural, she's totally at home on the air."

After four months on the show, Katie gave birth to her first child. Elinor "Ellie" Tully Monahan was born on July 23, 1991. Katie took two months off from work. On her first day back, Gumbel asked Katie if the baby slept through the show. "Only during your interviews," she joked.

HARD-HITTING INTERVIEWS

Katie's work at *Today* included serious interviews along with lighter pieces. She quickly became known for her hard-hitting questions. She never tiptoed around topics; she asked questions that were straight to the point and often tough to answer.

In October 1992, the presidential elections were drawing near. That became an important month for Katie and the *Today* show. She had to prepare numerous interviews on many serious topics. A week after interviewing President Bush at the White House, Katie spoke with Vice President Dan Quayle, who was campaigning for Bush. After Bill Clinton won the election in November, Katie was the first person to interview the new first lady—Hillary Rodham Clinton.

After her first year with *Today*, Katie received a hefty pay raise. Newspapers reported that she was making more than $1 million a

> **"The hard part is finding a flaw [in Katie]. She's the everything gal. She's an apple a day. She's real, she's natural, she's totally at home on the air."**
>
> — TOM SHALES,
> TV CRITIC

After Bill Clinton was elected president in 1992, Katie was the first person to interview the new first lady—Hillary Rodham Clinton.

year. Despite her newfound fame, Katie still felt the same as she had before the show. "My social circle hasn't changed. The idea of dumping my friends for fancier friends is so gross!" she told *People* magazine. "Who would want to do that? I'm not into flamboyant socializing."

On *Today,* Gumbel and Katie had a well-balanced working relationship on air, even though they were never best friends. While Katie was fun-loving and relaxed, Gumbel was serious and stiff. They respected each other's journalistic styles, however, and Katie could not imagine the *Today* show without him. "I think we complement each other," she said. "I'm not at my best when Bryant isn't next to me, and I don't think he's at his best when I'm not there to give him a hard time or make fun of him or make sure he's not taking himself oh-too-seriously." Viewers agreed—they loved their playful interaction.

As promised, Katie got to cover as many serious segments as Gumbel did. She was especially committed to women's issues and women's health concerns. Still, Katie liked to mix it up. During one show, she spoke with the director of the National Institutes of Health, and later exchanged jokes with comedian Jerry Seinfeld. According to one media analyst:

> Katie broke the mold in terms of what it meant to be an anchor on a morning show. Until Katie came along, all the previous anchors conformed to sexual stereotypes as to the division of labor. The man did the hard news and sports, and the woman did the women's sphere—child rearing, clothes, and food. Katie smashed those stereotypes. She and Bryant shared everything. She was the first modern woman on morning TV.

NETWORK COMPETITION

After a few years on *Today*, Katie added another job to her already busy work schedule. She and news anchor Tom Brokaw paired up for a new weekly television program on NBC called *Now with Tom Brokaw and Katie Couric*. Despite its meaty reporting, *Now* never got good enough ratings to challenge competitive newsmagazine programs. CBS's *60 Minutes* held the spot as the most popular newsmagazine. By

While on Today, *Katie teamed up with news anchor Tom Brokaw (left) for a short-lived weekly television program called* Now with Tom Brokaw and Katie Couric.

November 1994, *Now* became part of *Dateline*. Katie went back to focusing on her work on the *Today* show, though she still did regular interviews for *Dateline*. Even without the added responsibilities of *Now,* Katie had plenty to keep her busy.

The two most popular early morning television programs, *Today* and *Good Morning America,* were fierce competitors. They often battled to get the same interviews first. Morning shows also competed with many prime-time newsmagazine shows, including *20/20* and *60 Minutes*. Katie was contending against many other women in the broadcasting business who were also tough news anchors, such as Barbara Walters, Diane

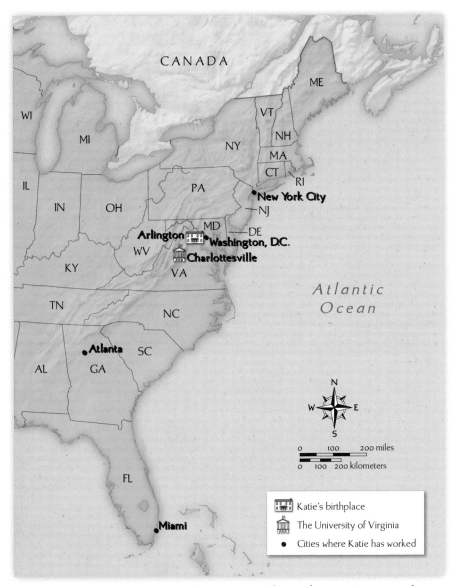

Katie has spent her entire life on the East Coast. She was born in Virginia, and even went to college there. An early reporting job took Katie as far south as Miami, Florida, but after a stint in Washington, D.C., she settled in New York City.

Advice for a Young Reporter

When Katie appeared on *The Larry King Show,* a caller asked her to give some advice for aspiring reporters. Katie answered:

"I think that probably the best advice I could give is that you should get some on-the-job experience. You know, internships were not that prevalent when I was in college; but I worked at radio stations in Washington every summer while I was at the University of Virginia. By the time I graduated, news directors and other people thought, 'Wow, she's got some serious work experience; and she's just out of college.' ...You have to be willing to start at the bottom and sweep the floors, and make coffee, and take advantage of where you are. Be willing to come in extra hours; even come in on weekends. Follow reporters around so you can watch the really good ones at work; and learn from them."

Sawyer, and Jane Pauley. Like Katie, Pauley had been a *Today* anchor and had also anchored *Dateline.*

Meanwhile, Katie was trying to balance her career with being a wife and mom. She wanted to spend as much time as she could with her daughter and Jay, but work often interfered. Katie understood the value of a strong family. Very soon, that strength would be put to the ultimate test. ❖

Katie frequently co-hosted NBC's coverage of Macy's Thanksgiving Day Parade in New York City. Here she's joined by Al Roker (left) and Matt Lauer (right).

CHAPTER SEVEN

JUGGLING ACT

KATIE HAD BEEN LIVING IN AN APARTMENT IN Manhattan with daughter Ellie during the week while Jay worked in Washington, D.C. In May 1994, after Jay took a job with a Manhattan law firm, Katie found a new apartment in New York City. For the first time since Katie started at the *Today* show, the whole family would be living together under one roof.

Still, Katie's life remained hectic. She had to be ready to leave for the studio at 5:00 in the morning. When her limousine pulled up at the NBC studios, fans were already waiting for her to sign autographs. After the show went off the air at 9:00, Katie continued working into the afternoon. She had to study for upcoming interviews and review material for the next day's show.

Although a nanny took care of Ellie during the day, Katie tried to devote her off-work hours to her daughter. As with all toddlers, there were nights when Ellie was up sick or restless. The next morning, Katie dragged herself to work exhausted. Occasionally, Ellie and the nanny would pop in to visit Katie at her NBC office. Ellie would color pictures until noon. Then Katie would sneak away for a quick lunch with her daughter. Maintaining a high-profile career and a happy family became a desperate juggling act for Katie.

In the summer of 1995, Katie revealed to her viewers that she and Jay were expecting their second child. Almost overnight, she became a fashion symbol for pregnant women everywhere. Expectant mothers called the show to find out where Katie had gotten her outfit or jewelry. On January 5, 1996—two

World Traveler

Her job as a journalist gives Katie lots of opportunities for travel. Covering the Olympic Games helped her see much of the world, including Barcelona, Spain (1992); Atlanta, Georgia (1996); Sydney, Australia (2000); Salt Lake City, Utah (2002); Athens, Greece (2004); and Torino, Italy (2006).

The Today *show team (with Olympic mascots) broadcast from Athens in 2004.*

Katie interviewed Bob Dole and Bill Clinton (pictured) during the presidential election of 1996. Both men had to answer hard-hitting questions.

days before Katie's 39th birthday—she gave birth to her second daughter, Caroline Couric Monahan. After a brief, two-month maternity leave, Katie was back at work. She and Jay continued to struggle with the increasing difficulties of building high-profile careers while caring for two young children. They decided to hire another nanny to help with little Carrie. This second nanny got up with the baby at night so that Katie could get the rest she needed to get up before 5:00 the next morning.

TOUGH QUESTIONS

In the summer of 1996, Katie was busy planning coverage of the upcoming presidential election. In an interview with Bob Dole, Katie drew the Republican candidate into a heated discussion about the tobacco industry. Dole had accepted campaign contributions from tobacco companies and had made an absurd claim that nicotine was not addictive. During the interview, Katie gave Dole a chance to respond to stories in the media about his comments. At one point, he said, "I've said, I don't know whether it's addictive. I'm not a doctor. I'm not a scientist. People shouldn't smoke, young or old. Now what else do you do?"

Katie then pointed out that Dr. C. Everett Koop, a highly respected professor at Dartmouth Medical School and a Dole supporter, had also criticized Dole's comments on tobacco. Katie used this information to prove that it was not just the media that opposed his comments. Dole stuck by his beliefs. "Dr. Koop, you know, he watches the liberal media, and he—," Dole began. "He's brainwashed?" Katie interrupted. Dole tried to catch himself. "[He] probably got carried away," he clarified. "Probably a little bit." The interview, which put Dole on the spot, was one of Katie's many defining moments as a hard-hitting journalist.

Some people found Katie's tough interviewing style abrasive. Her fans and co-anchors liked the way she fearlessly asked the questions everyone wanted to hear. Matt Lauer, a *Today* show news anchor, applauded Katie for the tough way she conducted her interviews. He said:

It's impossible for politicians not to be charmed by her. Then, all of a sudden, just when they're feeling real comfortable and they're sinking into their chair, the next thing you know, Pow! Right in the kisser!

TENSIONS ON THE SET

During the fall of 1996, things began to get stressful on the *Today* show set. Bryant Gumbel had accepted a job with rival network CBS. He would soon be leaving the show. Then, in October, producer Jeff Zucker was diagnosed with colon cancer. Katie quickly snapped into action and did all she could to help Zucker deal with the crisis. Katie researched the disease and the various treatment options. She even located the best cancer specialist in New York. As Zucker underwent surgery and chemotherapy treatments, Katie remained a devoted friend and colleague. Just two months after surgery, Zucker was back at work, and Katie could breathe a sigh of relief.

When Bryant Gumbel left Today *in 1997, Matt Lauer took his spot as co-anchor. Matt's easy-going personality was a perfect fit with Katie's laid-back style.*

When Gumbel announced that he was leaving the show, NBC executives offered Katie the chance to be sole anchor of *Today*. She preferred to have a co-host, though. Matt Lauer, who had reported the news on *Today* since 1994, got the job.

In December, Zucker put together a tribute to Gumbel's 15 years on the program. Celebrities such as First Lady Hillary Clinton and former president George Bush, as well as actors John Travolta, Tom Cruise, and Sandra Bullock sent video tributes that were aired during Gumbel's last broadcast on January 3, 1997.

Matt Lauer

Born on December 30, 1957, Matt Lauer is best known as co-anchor of the *Today* show. He grew up in Greenwich, Connecticut, and later attended Ohio University. In 1979, he left college just four credits shy of graduating. However, he finished those credits in 1997 (while he was working at the *Today* show) to receive a degree in communications. Between 1979 and 1994, Lauer held a variety of broadcasting jobs—from reporter to host—for several TV stations. In 1994, he became a full-time news anchor for the *Today* show. When Bryant Gumbel left in 1997, Lauer took his spot as official co-anchor. Lauer's easy-going personality and obvious rapport with Katie helped his popularity soar. Today, he co-anchors the show with former *Who Wants to Be a Millionaire* and *The View* host Meredith Vieira.

The Today *show cast had a tradition of dressing up in costumes every Halloween. In 2004, (left to right) Katie dressed as Donald Trump, Al Roker was Oprah Winfrey, Matt Lauer was Paris Hilton, and Ann Curry was Tina Turner.*

Holding up glasses of champagne, the *Today* staff toasted Gumbel and gave him a standing ovation. With his departure, a new era was dawning on the *Today* show. Matt Lauer's on-air style resembled Katie's—laid-back and informal. She and Lauer had real chemistry. They seemed to get along and were always joking with each other. Their on-air friendship sent ratings through the roof.

Each morning, Katie, Lauer, and the show's weatherman, Al Roker, enjoyed mixing with the crowd that gathered outside the studio. Even in the bitter cold New York winters, people huddled

Morning News Trailblazer

NBC pioneered the morning news when it launched the *Today* show on January 14, 1952. For the first 48 years, the show ran in a standard, two-hour format. Then, in October 2000, the network added a third hour, making *Today* the only three-hour nationally broadcast morning show. The show extended to four hours in September 2007.

The live *Today* broadcast features breaking news, weather reports, and interviews with celebrities from politics, business, media, entertainment, and sports. For 11 consecutive years, while Katie was co-anchor, the show was America's overwhelming morning favorite. In June 1994, *Today* moved from its longtime home at New York's 30 Rockefeller Plaza to a stunning new site right next door. The glass-walled, ground-floor studio sits at the corner of 49th Street and Rockefeller Plaza. Each day, hundreds of fans peer into the windows and become part of that

day's broadcast. After the show, Katie often went outside to shake hands with her fans and sign autographs.

outside the glass windows, watching the *Today* set and waving at the cameras. During the show, the *Today* staff joined the crowd outside, shaking hands and chatting with fans. Oftentimes, Katie went back outside after the show was over to sign autographs and take pictures with fans. Jeff Zucker said:

> *She is the kid on the playground, not the dolled-up, glamorous, ready-for-prime-time anchor. Perhaps we defined morning television for the nineties, by mistake, when we found Katie.*

The show's popularity continued to grow. By 1997, more than 10 million people around the world were watching the *Today* show. For them, Katie had become like an old friend.

TROUBLING NEWS

Meanwhile, Jay had accepted a new position as a legal analyst for the MSNBC network. From time to time, he would appear on Geraldo Rivera's show, *Rivera Live,* as a guest commentator. Then, Jay began suffering from health problems. Day after day, he felt tired and achy. At first, he blamed his fatigue on his frequent traveling—he had been flying back and forth between California and New York. Katie and Jay both hoped his health would improve when his schedule lightened up. After finally deciding that he should go to a doctor, Katie and Jay were totally unprepared for what the doctors would find. ❖

After Jay died in 1998, Katie led a crusade against colon cancer. She works hard to keep his memory alive for her daughters.

CHAPTER EIGHT

KATIE'S CRUSADE

IN APRIL 1997, JAY'S DOCTORS MADE A SHOCKING discovery. He was diagnosed with colon cancer. That was the same disease that *Today* show producer Jeff Zucker had battled and defeated just a year earlier. Katie was stunned. "The two most important men in my life getting it was just so hard to believe," she said. "I would wake up every day and say, 'I can't believe Jay got it.'"

Just a few weeks later, Jay underwent surgery to have the cancer removed. If it is detected early, colon cancer is a curable disease, but it is unpredictable. Zucker had been lucky. In Jay's case, the cancer continued to ravage his body after the surgery. The disease was in its advanced stages and had already spread to his other organs.

Throughout the summer and fall of 1997, Jay underwent chemotherapy and radiation treatments. Doctors hoped to slow down the spread of cancer in his body. Like most people who have these treatments, he lost his hair. Cancer and its treatments are brutal on the body. Jay grew increasingly weak, thin, and pale. Watching Jay slowly deteriorate was devastating for Katie and the girls. Jay was always optimistic and talked about the future. He never complained or showed self-pity. Katie, too, stayed positive. "I never wanted to give up hope, for Jay or for my children," she later said. When Ellie would ask if her dad was going to die, Katie answered as honestly as she could. "I really hope not, sweetie, but I'm not sure," she told Ellie. "He

In 1996, Katie and Ellie (center) were all smiles during an outing with a friend. When Jay became ill, Ellie had to face the possibility of losing her father.

has a very difficult illness, but his doctors are doing everything they possibly can."

A FIGHT TO THE END

Katie struggled to come to terms with what was happening to her family. Jay was only in his early forties. People just aren't supposed to die that young. A young woman isn't supposed to be a widow. Little girls shouldn't have to grow up without their father. Katie spent long hours researching treatment alternatives with little success. It was more than frustrating. Katie had made a career of finding answers. Now, when it was a matter of life or death, there were no answers to be found. Katie talked to dozens of doctors and biotech companies—laboratories that specialize in researching and treating diseases. When one didn't have the answer, she moved to another, desperate to find the key to saving her husband's life. After months of fruitless exploration, she was scared, exhausted, and at the end of her rope.

> "I never wanted to give up hope, for Jay or for my children."
>
> – KATIE COURIC

On January 24, 1998, Jay collapsed on the bathroom floor of the family's apartment. He was rushed to the hospital where he later died with Katie at his side. He was just 42 years old. Jay's death was heartbreaking for Katie. Although she'd interviewed people who had gone through tragedies, she had never experienced a personal tragedy as deep as this before. Until the bitter end, she had held out hope that doctors would find a way to save her husband. Publicly, she had talked very little about his

Learning to Heal

Children who have a sick parent can feel very isolated, like no one can understand what they are going through. During Jay's illness and after his death, Katie and the girls went to psychologists for counseling to help them deal with the pain of watching someone they love suffer and die. A representative from CancerCare, a nonprofit organization, suggested an exercise for Ellie's class called the worry cup. In the exercise, each child puts a penny in a cup and talks about what they're worried about. Ellie found out that a lot of the kids in her class were worried about something. It helped her feel less alone.

suffering or how his disease had affected their family. Now, she had to face Jay's death with the whole world watching.

FIGHTING BACK

Katie took a month off from *Today* to spend time at home with 6-year-old Ellie and 2-year-old Carrie. She started putting together a book of all the letters people wrote to her about Jay. She hopes the letters will help her girls feel like they know a lot about their father and what an outstanding person he was. She also wrote the girls a letter all about their parents' courtship—how Katie and Jay met and why she fell in love with him. "The idea is that when they're older they can read about him and appreciate him," Katie explained. "I've asked people to write to my girls, and I've received the most beautiful letters."

Returning to work was not easy for Katie, but she knew that it would help her family get back into a normal routine. At home, her life had drastically changed. She was now a single parent of two young girls. Jay was no longer there to be a part of the day-to-day routine. The house was empty without him. Katie missed his friendship and support.

THE SHOW MUST GO ON

Katie was always very private. She never shared the full story of Jay's illness and death with her television audience. Although many other news anchors wanted to interview her after the ordeal, Katie offered few interviews. Even though there were many days she felt like breaking down, she had to be strong and find a way to keep smiling. "It's very hard to live out a personal tragedy on national television," she said. "Every day my heart was breaking."

> **"It's very hard to live out a personal tragedy on national television. Every day my heart was breaking."**
>
> – KATIE COURIC

One of the first times Katie mentioned her struggle was when she was honored at the Avon Women of Enterprise Awards in June 1998. In her speech, she said:

> *How do you go on when fate delivers such a crushing blow that causes permanent damage to your heart? I've often wondered. … I do it because I have two girls who*

are depending on me to show them what you have to do
when life throws you a major curve ball.

Shortly after this speech, Katie began to fight back. She started to talk more openly about colon cancer. She thought maybe she could spare someone else the pain Jay had suffered. "I can't bear to see other families going through this," she said.

Katie and the *Today* show staff pulled together all the information they had found about the deadly disease. Then, in September, Katie presented a five-part series on colon cancer on the *Today* show. The series, "Confronting Colon Cancer," won

In 2000, Katie testified before a Senate Special Committee on Aging about the importance of colorectal cancer screenings.

A Public-Health Hero

After Jay's death, Katie became determined to help in the fight against cancer. In 2000, she cofounded the National Colorectal Cancer Research Alliance (NCCRA) with the Entertainment Industry Foundation (EIF). Katie and the EIF also led the effort to create a center for colon cancer screening and treatment. The Jay Monahan Center for Gastrointestinal Health opened at New York-Presbyterian Weill Cornell Medical Center in 2004. The center, named after Katie's late husband, focuses on both preventative screening and treatment. "Katie Couric has courageously and unselfishly promoted the power of prevention to save lives," said Dr. Howard Koh from the Harvard School of Public Health. "We all honor her as a public-health hero."

the prestigious Peabody Award. Katie hoped to impress upon her viewers how important it was to get regular checkups. If Jay had caught his cancer earlier, he may have survived. Katie came up with

"I can't bear to see other families going through this."

– KATIE COURIC

a blunt catchphrase to grab people's attention: "Get your butt to the doctor! It could save your life." The series was a hit with viewers. The NBC network decided to feature part of it on *NBC Nightly News,* as well as on MSNBC.

TV BIDDING WARS

Not long after Katie returned to *Today*, rumors began circu-
lating about a secret NBC plot to replace her. In response, the
Globe tabloid paper wrote an article that mentioned the flood of
offers Katie had received from NBC's competitors. Her contract
was set to expire in July 1998. Other networks were dying for
the chance to snag the star anchor.

> "And now [begins]
> the Battle for Katie
> Couric ..."
>
> – VERNE GAY,
> NEWSDAY'S TV CRITIC

On June 17, 1998, the *Wall Street
Journal* ran a story under the headline "Today Co-Anchor Expected to
Enter TV Bidding Wars." The story
revealed that Katie might be considered for a slot on *60 Minutes*, and at
least one network had offered Katie the chance at her own television show. As one TV critic proclaimed, "And now [begins]
the Battle for Katie Couric ..."

Katie considered walking away from *Today* if the network
didn't offer her enough money to stay. She was not being greedy,
just asking for what she felt she deserved. She explained:

> *The network makes a lot of [money] off us. My
> personality plays a role in the show's success, not that
> it would collapse if I left. But people have this strong
> connection to you and form these bonds with you that
> are almost familial. It takes a long time to win the
> audience's trust and affection.*

She made a valid point. When Katie joined *Today* in 1991, the
show was only making a modest profit. It consistently ranked

second in the ratings behind *Good Morning America*. Eight years later, the *Today* show was reeling in millions of dollars and had blasted way ahead of *Good Morning America* in the ratings. Clearly Katie was worth a lot of money. Her bosses at NBC agreed—they offered her a new $7-million-a-year contract.

Meanwhile, Katie continued to promote cancer awareness. In March 2000, she underwent a colonoscopy on the air. Her bold attitude inspired many others to get checked. Medical researchers reported a 20 percent increase in screenings nationwide and dubbed the phenomenon "the Couric Effect." Not long after, cancer struck another violent blow. In October 2001, Katie's sister Emily died of pancreatic cancer. Katie delivered the eulogy at the funeral. "I just want you to know I will always be proud to say, 'I am Emily Couric's sister,'" she told the other mourners.

In October 2001, Emily Couric died of pancreatic cancer. Before she was diagnosed with the deadly disease, Katie's sister had served as a state senator in Virginia. She was considered a sure-win candidate for lieutenant governor.

SHARING TRAGEDY

As a broadcast journalist, Katie often has to cover national tragedies. Just as she was recovering from her personal tragedy, the country mourned the students who were gunned down at Columbine High School in Littleton, Colorado. On April 20, 1999, two students armed with guns and bombs entered the school and opened fire. They killed 13 people and wounded more than 30 others before taking their own lives. Katie was one of the first national news broadcasters to arrive on the scene. Her own experience with losing Jay made her more compassionate toward people who have lost a loved one too soon. Interviewing parents and students who had lost someone in the shooting spree—a son, a daughter, a friend—was extremely emotional for her, as well as for viewers of the *Today* show. Katie understood that it took great courage for those family members and friends to appear on television.

That same year, Katie published her first children's book, *The Brand New Kid*. The tragic events at Columbine High School inspired Katie to write the story. Investigations into the shootings revealed that the students who opened fire had been taunted by other classmates. Katie's book is about Lazlo, a new kid at school. Lazlo, who is from Hungary, gets teased by the other students because he looks different and talks with an accent. Katie hopes the book will encourage children to talk about how to deal with differences among people.

Katie's ability to relate to everyday Americans made her an incredible asset to the NBC network. At $7 million a year, she was earning a higher salary than many of her male colleagues.

Queen of the Crossover

Writing children's books isn't the only way Katie has branched off from TV journalism. Over the years, she has made a number of crossovers from hard-hitting journalist to TV celebrity. She was the voice of news reporter Katie Current in the animated film *Shark Tale*. She also made a cameo appearance as a prison

In 1992, Katie (far right) was among several real-life female newscasters who were invited to a baby shower for fictional TV journalist Murphy Brown.

guard in *Austin Powers in Goldmember*. In addition to guest-starring on the sitcom *Murphy Brown*, Katie played herself in an episode of *Will & Grace* and appeared in an episode of *Cheers*. Katie also co-hosted NBC's live coverage of the Macy's Thanksgiving Day Parade from 1991 to 2005.

She made more than Dan Rather from the *CBS Evening News* and Ed Bradley from *60 Minutes*. When her contract was due to expire in May 2002, she was looking to do even better. There was no doubt that executives at NBC wanted to keep Katie on

Today. They did not want to lose their star anchor to a competing network. They were ready to pay Katie to stay. Industry analysts thought she might get as much as the $10 million a year NBC paid Tom Brokaw.

As it turned out, Katie's offer exceeded everyone's wildest imaginations. NBC agreed to pay her the massive sum of $65 million over the next four and a half years, or about $15 million a year. With this raise, Katie became the highest-paid journalist in the history of television news. In 2004, she published a second children's book with another valuable lesson for kids.

Katie has published two books for children—both with valuable life lessons. The Blue Ribbon Day *teaches children how to deal with disappointment.*

In *The Blue Ribbon Day*, Katie encourages children to deal positively with disappointment. She also continued to support cancer awareness. In October 2005, Katie broadcast her own mammogram on the *Today* show, drawing awareness to the issue of breast cancer. She hoped her openness would create "the Couric Effect" for breast cancer screening.

Then, on April 6, 2006, Katie dropped a bombshell on her *Today* audience. She announced that, after 15 years, she was leaving the show. She was taking over as anchor of the *CBS Evening News*. Katie would be the first woman to be the solo anchor of an evening newscast. NBC offered her $20 million a year to stay at *Today*, but Katie felt like it was time to move on to something new. She told her viewers:

> *After listening to my heart and my gut, two things that have served me pretty well in the past, I will be leaving* Today *at the end of May. I really feel as if we've become friends through the years. Sometimes I think change is a good thing. Although it may be terrifying to get out of your comfort zone, it's very exciting to start a new chapter in your life.* ❖

After 15 years, Katie bid farewell to the Today *show*.
She was heading to the CBS Evening News, *where she
would be America's first female solo anchor.*

CHAPTER NINE

FLYING SOLO

T HE DECISION TO LEAVE *TODAY* WAS VERY TOUGH
for Katie. She had such a connection with her viewers.
When she said good-bye, Katie told her fans:

*It may sound corny, but I really feel as if we've become
friends through the years. ... You've been with me during
a lot of good times and some very difficult times as well.
And, hopefully, I've been there for you.*

It was a tough choice but one she felt she had to make. Katie
had made history. Successful news anchors such as Barbara
Walters, Connie Chung, and Elizabeth Vargas have all been co-
anchors of nightly newscasts. Katie was the first woman to regularly anchor a broadcast network's weeknight newscast alone.
She would also contribute to *60 Minutes* and star in her own
prime-time specials.

BROADCASTING PIONEER

Katie's new job was well deserved, but it offered a new set of challenges. On the set of *Today*, she kidded with Matt Lauer, goofed around with celebrities, and dressed up in Halloween costumes. The evening news was all about serious journalism. It would be a giant shift for Katie and her viewers.

Katie was excited about her new serious role. For 15 years, she had dealt with the nickname "America's sweetheart," but she never liked the idea of being cute. "It makes me kind of puke," she admitted. Her audience and the general public thought it fit, though. Now Katie had to convince everyone that she was the

Katie's CBS premiere on September 5 drew a whopping 13.6 million viewers—a much bigger audience than the competing networks' evening news programs.

right person for a serious news job. Some people felt that she was too perky to take the seat of a nightly anchor. Several factors were working in her favor, though. Katie had always excelled at interviews and live news—critical skills for any anchor.

During a time when anchoring was changing dramatically, Katie could be a refreshing presence. Bob Schieffer, the man whose spot Katie was taking, had set a terrific example for her. He anchored in a down-to-earth manner, much like Katie. He made the evening news more inviting by chatting with reporters. Schieffer believed in Katie's abilities as an anchor. When some people expressed concerns that the *CBS Evening News* would be become "fluffy" on her watch, Schieffer disagreed. "I don't think that's what Katie wants to do," he said. "She's a serious person. She didn't come to CBS to put on an entertainment spectacular. She wants to show she's a good journalist."

> **"[Katie's] a serious person. She didn't come to CBS to put on an entertainment spectacular. She wants to show she's a good journalist."**
>
> – BOB SCHIEFFER

A NEW KIND OF ANCHOR

Katie wanted to fit the part of a serious news anchor while still bringing a bit of her personality to the nightly news. Instead of the stuffy "Good evening" salutation, Katie addressed her audience with an informal "Hi, everyone." Most anchors use the traditional "Good evening" introduction. Katie thought this type of a greeting was too uptight for her. As of the first week,

Katie's new approach seemed to have worked. Her premiere on September 5 drew 13.6 million viewers. That was much better than the competing networks' evening news programs. At the end of her first week, CBS had won the network-news ratings race with an average of 10.2 million viewers. It was the first time the network ranked first since June of 2001.

CBS won the week, but right from the start Katie was losing viewers every night. On Wednesday, the day after her debut, the numbers dropped to 10.3 million. On Thursday night they were down to 9.5 million. Her audience had shrunk to 7.4 million on Friday. *Evening News* producer Rome Hartman was not worried, though. In fact, he felt encouraged by the new viewers Katie had drawn. "We had millions more people," he said, "and millions of different people watching the *Evening News*." With Katie, there had been a 55 percent increase in viewers between the ages of 18 and 49. This is the key group that networks and advertisers try to reach. Before she took over at the *Evening News,* the majority of viewers were over 60 years old. However, it would take weeks or months for real conclusions to be made.

UNDER THE MICROSCOPE

Meanwhile, the media was scrutinizing Katie's performance. They dissected her outfits and criticized her heavy makeup. Katie hoped viewers would focus on the substance of her reporting over her style. If she was annoyed by the critiques on her hair and wardrobe Katie kept a sense of humor about it. "As long as they talk about Brian Williams's tie and Charlie Gibson's suit, I'm fine with [the comments]," she joked.

The media's treatment of Katie was not a big surprise. According to ex-CNN anchor Judy Woodruff, it was business as usual. She explained:

When you're a woman on television, no matter how serious your assignment is, some people will be judging you on how you look. It's just the way it is. You work around it. … People commented on everything from the length of my skirt to my hairstyle to what kind of jewelry I wore. It's part and parcel of how women are seen in our society.

Katie tried not to focus on how her looks were being scrutinized. She had other concerns. Unfortunately, she couldn't keep the *CBS Evening News* at number one. By October, the program was back where it had started—in third place. Producer Rome Hartman was beginning to get concerned about the collapse in Katie's ratings.

On one occasion, Katie introduced a story about Arnold Schwarzenegger by imitating "Ah-nuld's" funny way of talking. Another time, she handed a pair of pink slippers to correspondent Steve Hartman after he did a feature on a Texas sheriff who forced his prisoners to wear pink. The network never complained about these amusing tidbits. After all, clever quips had been Katie's trademark. They were part of the reason why America had fallen in love with her.

> **"As long as they talk about Brian Williams's tie and Charlie Gibson's suit, I'm fine with [the comments]."**
>
> – KATIE COURIC

Her natural, witty personality was not winning over the night-time audience, though. Ratings continued to drop. As the critical February network sweeps drew closer, Katie started acting differently. Her loose and smiley demeanor seemed to tighten up. She even dropped her breezy "Hi, everyone" opener and replaced it with a more proper "Hello, everyone."

> **"Some people are rooting for me to fail."**
>
> – KATIE COURIC

In 15 years at *Today*, Katie had always come out on top in the sweeps, but the February 2007

Network Sweeps

There are four "sweeps" periods during the year—in November, February, May, and July. During these four-week sweeps periods, the advertising rates for a network's shows are set with sponsors and advertisers. It is crucial that a network get the highest ratings possible during these sweeps, so that they can charge higher rates from advertisers. If a network can win the sweeps, it can charge higher advertising rates, thus generating higher profits. Networks often roll out eye-catching specials and dramatic TV show episodes, such as season-ending cliff hangers, hoping to boost ratings. It was critical for Katie to do well during the sweeps. She knew that if she failed to bring in more viewers, she might be replaced.

Katie continued to use her tough interviewing skills on the CBS Evening News, *where she sat down with government officials such as Secretary of State Condoleezza Rice.*

results revealed a turn of events. In her first six months at the *Evening News,* Katie had failed to increase the number of viewers who watched the program. The gains she made during her first few months had slipped through her fingers. The critics were ready to pounce. Once again, Katie felt like everyone was against her. "Some people are rooting for me to fail," she said.

Katie's career as a solo anchor has not been all bad, though. She has covered important events like a veteran. In November 2006, she anchored from Amman, Jordan, covering President George W. Bush's summit meeting with Iraqi Prime Minister Nouri al-Maliki. In December of that year, she covered the death of former President Gerald Ford and, four days later, the execution of Saddam Hussein.

In 2007, Katie covered the Virginia Tech shootings for the *CBS Evening News* and did a one-hour special on the event. She also anchored the award-winning prime-time special "Flashpoint," the story of CBS News correspondent Kimberly Dozier, her colleagues, and the U.S. soldiers she was with when they were victims of a car bomb attack in Iraq.

Katie covered the historic presidential race of 2008, anchoring the *CBS Evening News* and live coverage of the primaries. She also conducted a critically acclaimed series of in-depth inter-

In August 2008, Katie covered the Democratic National Convention in Denver, Colorado. Here, she interviews Party Chairman Howard Dean.

Katie spearheaded the "Stand Up to Cancer" campaign. She and anchors from rival networks hosted an hour-long television special on September 5, 2008.

views for the *CBS Evening News* called "Primary Questions." She asked 10 questions of the 10 candidates who were then in the race for presidency. The questions helped define the views, character, and leadership qualities of the candidates. Her tough questions left some candidates stumbling for a response.

On May 28, 2008, Katie and her ABC News and NBC News competitors Charles Gibson and Brian Williams announced a first-ever, joint-network effort to fight cancer. Called "Stand Up to Cancer," the program would air on all three networks' morning news broadcasts. All money raised during the one-hour, commercial-free program on September 5 would be donated to groundbreaking cancer research.

In 2008, Katie and her daughter Ellie attended a screening of Mamma Mia! *hosted by the Breast Cancer Research Foundation.*

LOOKING TO TOMORROW

There was some talk among CBS executives of replacing Katie with another anchor, but factors other than just ratings need to be taken into consideration. For example, people are not gathering around the TV set right after dinner at home anymore. Ratings for all evening newscasts are dwindling, and the total number of viewers for all networks' evening newscasts is expected to keep dropping.

No matter what happens, Katie has plenty of options. She continues to serve as an anchor for *60 Minutes*. In fact, she has talked about doing more pieces for the show, and could make a permanent move to the newsmagazine program if things don't work out on the *Evening News*. Still, that type of change would be difficult for Katie. She has spent a lifetime striving to fulfill her father's dream for her—to sit in the chair once occupied by the great Walter Cronkite. When she was a little girl, Katie's father told her that she was destined for greatness. She believed him and surpassed his wildest expectations.

Along the way, Katie has conquered tremendous obstacles. She made it to the top, but she had to fight the entire way. Katie is used to being under fire, and she is not likely to give up now. When CNN founder Reese Schonfeld said of Katie, "I never want to see her on the air again," she could have walked away from a career in TV journalism, but she did not. When her bosses wouldn't take her seriously or give her the big stories, Katie might have quit, but she did not.

Throughout the world, Katie Couric has become an icon for ambition, courage, and determination. She has set the bar high for women everywhere—challenging them to achieve their wildest goals and dreams. Her crusade against cancer has undoubtedly saved many lives. With many more years of success ahead of her, Katie is always looking to tomorrow. Whatever challenges sit on the horizon, she has proven she can handle both triumph and strife with grace … and a warm smile. ❖

TIME LINE

1957 Katherine Anne (Katie) is born to John and
Elinor Couric on January 7.

1975 Katie graduates from Yorktown High School
in Arlington, Virginia.

1979 Katie receives a bachelor's degree with
honor from the University of Virginia in
Charlottesville; takes a job as a desk assistant
at the ABC News bureau in Washington, D.C.

1980 Katie accepts a position as an assignment
editor at CNN with its Washington bureau.

1984 Katie becomes a reporter at WTVJ in Miami
and later wins an award for her series on child
pornography.

1986 Katie returns to Washington, D.C., and
becomes a reporter at WRC-TV, the local NBC
television affiliate.

1989 Katie wins a local Emmy Award
and an Associated Press Award
for her segment about a dating
service for the disabled; becomes
a Pentagon reporter for NBC;
marries lawyer Jay Monahan.

1990 In May, Katie becomes a
national correspondent for the *Today* show in
New York City.

1991 Katie becomes *Today* show co-host with Bryant Gumbel on April 5; gives birth to Elinor Tully (Ellie) Monahan on July 23.

1996 Katie covers the Olympics and the U.S. presidential election; gives birth to Caroline Couric (Carrie) Monahan on January 5. *Today* show producer Jeff Zucker is diagnosed with and recovers from colon cancer.

1997 After Bryant Gumbel resigns, Matt Lauer joins Katie as co-anchor of *Today*. Katie's husband Jay is diagnosed with colon cancer.

1998 Jay dies on January 27; Katie creates a series on colon cancer for *Today* called "Confronting Colon Cancer," which wins a Peabody Award.

1999 Katie is named "Hero of the Year" by *Life* magazine; rates as top journalist in the *Good Housekeeping* "Most Admired Women" poll; is voted one of 10 "Women's Health Heroes" by *American Health* magazine.

2000 Katie has an on-air colonoscopy, inspiring others to have the test, and cofounds the National Colorectal Cancer Research Alliance (NCCRA). Her children's book *The Brand New Kid* is published.

2001 *TV Guide* names Katie Best News Person of the Year. Katie's sister Emily dies of pancreatic cancer on October 18.

2004 Katie publishes her second children's book, *The Blue Ribbon Day*.

2005 Katie undergoes a mammogram on the *Today* show, hoping to encourage other women to have the test.

2006 On April 6, Katie announces she will be leaving the *Today* show after 15 years. Her last day is on May 31. Katie takes a job with the *CBS Evening News*, becoming the first ever  solo female news anchor. Her premiere on the *CBS Evening News* tops the ratings with 13.6 million viewers.

2008 Katie helps develop the idea for a fund-raising event called "Stand Up to Cancer." The television program airs simultaneously on ABC, NBC, and CBS on September 5.

A CONVERSATION WITH
Maria Brennan

Maria Brennan is the president of American Women in Radio and Television (AWRT) and its sister foundation. She is also on the Women's Leadership Board at the John F. Kennedy School of Government at Harvard University. Here, Maria talks about Katie's influence.

Q. What are some of the challenges that women have had to overcome to succeed in broadcasting?

A. It's a very male-dominated field, [so] the obstacles are going to be greater. Plus there is often a higher degree of scrutiny of females in the media—from story lines and number of days off to skirt lengths and hairstyles. Dodging this and other demands, while trying to deliver substantive and timely stories, is not for everyone. Only the strong survive. Of course, having a great mind, talent, and determination helps, too.

Q. Why do you think it took so long for a woman to be chosen to solo anchor the news? Why was Katie first?

A. For the same reason it took us so long to get to vote. We may have been created equal, but we're not always treated that way.

There were [other female broadcasters who] helped pave the way for [Katie] to become the first [female] solo anchor. [Perhaps Katie was chosen because] she is a proven asset [and] women are historically strong at delivering ratings in all sorts of news formats.

Q. What skills does a news anchor, like Katie Couric, need to succeed?

A. Tremendous energy, a sharp mind, and unrelenting dedication [are essential to success]. [Being a news anchor] is difficult for many reasons—just try [to imagine] having to find [the right balance for being] viewed as credible, impartial, and yet 100 percent human.

Q. How is Katie's approach to the job different from that of the men who were anchors before her?

A. I see no differences in how she presents the news compared with others. However, she has managed to diversify the delivery methods of her newscasts through a post-show web cast, ultimately appealing to a younger, more tech-inclined demographic.

Q. Why did the media pay so much attention to Katie's hiring at CBS? Was the coverage fair?

A. Katie herself is newsworthy. She's more than a journalist and anchor; she's also a celebrity. She has a tremendous fan base. People like to follow her moves. And of course because she's a first, it becomes … a human interest story. Is the coverage of her fair? Not always. But fairness and story coverage do not always stand side by side.

Q. How do you think Katie has changed the career prospects for women in broadcasting?

A. I believe Couric's "first" will serve to help other women break into the media. It's [similar] to how other women before Katie helped create the inroads she could follow—woman such as Linda Ellerbee, Barbara Walters, Diane Sawyer, Cokie Roberts, and Connie Chung, just to name a few. There is also evidence [that she and other female broadcasters have influenced] college enrollment numbers—where women are outpacing men in choosing journalism as a career.

Q. Katie has been particularly active in raising awareness about cancer, and she did so in a very personal yet public way. Would you say her efforts have been effective, and if so, why?

A. Of course—she has taken what was once a taboo subject ... and put it in our living rooms and brought it to our dinner tables. Now, *colonoscopy* is a household word.

Q. What would you say have been Katie's greatest achievements so far?

A. There are so many, but perhaps her reporting [skills] and [charitable work in the fight against] colon cancer will be her greatest legacy.

GLOSSARY

adversity: misfortune, trouble, or disaster

affiliate: a member of a particular group (or television network), club, or association

agent: someone who is authorized to act on behalf of an artist, such as a writer or an actor

anchor: an on-air person who holds a newscast together

arrogant: overly proud and full of oneself

beat: a territory or area a reporter covers

briefing: a summary of the main points of an event

broadcast: a radio or TV program

catapulted: to have been suddenly thrown or thrust into a particular situation

co-anchor: an on-air person who shares the job of holding a newscast together

colonoscopy: a test that allows a doctor to look at the inner lining of a patient's large intestine

control room: a room from which engineers and production people control and direct a television or radio program

correspondent: a reporter who covers news from a distant place (outside of the studio)

corruption: deterioration of integrity, virtue, or moral principle

discrimination: the act of treating people differently based on race, sex, religion, age, or other difference

eclipsed: overshadowed

elite: a group set apart as special, influential, powerful, or the best

feminist: someone who supports and defends the rights of women

finesse: skillful, smooth handling of a situation

frivolous: of little importance

icon: someone masses of people look up to and respect

invasive: characterized by force or intrusion, as in a procedure that involves inserting a medical instrument into the body

journalist: someone who gathers and reports the news

live feed: recording of live television

network: a chain of television stations

pinnacle: highest point

profile: a short, vivid biography of someone

salutation: a greeting

segment: a part of a television program

sorority: a society or club of female students at a college

spontaneous: acting on impulse

stereotype: a generalization about someone based on opinion or conventional attitude

veteran: someone who has experience in a field

FOR MORE INFORMATION

Books and Other Resources

Banting, Erinn. *Katie Couric*. New York: Weigl Publishers, 2008.

Paprocki, Sherry Beck. *Katie Couric*. New York: Chelsea House Publishers, 2001.

Parish, James Robert. *Katie Couric: TV News Broadcaster*. New York: Ferguson, 2006.

Charlie Rose with Katie Couric and Matt Lauer. DVD: Charlie Rose, Inc., August 2006.

Web Sites

CBS News
www.cbsnews.com/sections/eveningnews/main3420.shtml
Visit this site to find out what's on tap for the nightly news, or watch videos on the top news stories. You can also join the conversation at the *CBS News* blog, Couric & Co.

The National Colorectal Cancer Research Alliance (NCCRA)
www.eifoundation.org/national/nccra/splash
This web site offers information about the National Colorectal Cancer Research Alliance (NCCRA), as well as the Entertainment Industry Foundation (EIF)—a charitable organization that raises awareness and funds for health, educational, and social issues.

SELECT BIBLIOGRAPHY
AND SOURCE NOTES

Klein, Edward. *Katie: the Real Story.* N.Y.: Crown Publishers, 2007.

Marin, Rick. "The Katie Factor." *Newsweek.* July 6, 1998.

Thomas, Marlo. *The Right Words at the Right Time.* N.Y.: Atria Books, 2002.

PAGE 2
Thomas, Marlo, *The Right Words at the Right Time.* N.Y.: Atria Books, 2002, p. 63

CHAPTER ONE
Page 8, line 11: Zoglin, Richard. "Katie Couric," *Time,* April 26, 2004

CHAPTER TWO
Page 13, line 8: Klein, Edward. *Katie: the Real Story.* N.Y.: Crown Publishers, 2007, p. 13
Page 14, line 4: Ibid., p. 14
Page 14, line 24: Thomas. *The Right Words at the Right Time,* pp. 61–63
Page 15, line 1: Ibid.
Page 16, line 4: Ibid.
Page 16, line 13: Ibid., p. 63
Page 16, line 25: Klein. *Katie: the Real Story,* p. 13
Page 19, line 3: Petrucelli, Alan W. "Down-to-Earth Katie Couric," *Working Mother,* July–August, 1996
Page 21, line 8: Klein. *Katie: the Real Story,* p. 22
Page 21, line 22: Ibid.
Page 22, sidebar: Grove, Lloyd. "Kiss of the Anchorwoman," *Vanity Fair,* August 1994

CHAPTER THREE
Page 25, line 12: Bumiller, Elisabeth.

"What You Don't Know about Katie Couric," *Good Housekeeping,* August 1, 1996
Page 26, line 8: Ibid.
Page 28, line 3: Klein. *Katie: the Real Story,* p. 5
Page 28, line 13: Ibid.

CHAPTER FOUR
Page 32, line 7: Klein. *Katie: the Real Story,* p. 28
Page 33, line 11: Ibid., p. 30
Page 34, line 9: Marin, Rick. "The Katie Factor," *Newsweek,* July 6, 1998
Page 36, line 11: Klein. *Katie: the Real Story,* p. 33
Page 36, line 24: Ibid., p. 34
Page 37, line 10: Ibid.
Page 37, line 16: Ibid.
Page 38, line 1: Ibid.
Page 39, line 6: Matusow, Barbara. "Up and at 'em Katie Couric climbs the anchor chain to a top job on NBC's 'Today'," *Chicago Tribune,* May 5, 1991

CHAPTER FIVE
Page 43, line 4: Klein. *Katie: the Real Story,* p. 49
Page 43, line 11: Ibid.
Page 46, sidebar: Ibid., p. 59
Page 46, line 3: Ibid.
Page 47, line 17: Flander, Judy. "Catching Up with Katie Couric," *Saturday Evening Post,* September–October, 1992
Page 48, line 4: Romano, Lois. "Stories That Changed Lives," *Redbook,* October 1991

CHAPTER SIX
Page 51, line 10: Schwarzbaum, Lisa. "Katie Did It," *Entertainment Weekly,* July 31, 1992

Page 52, line 3: Williams, Lena. "The Woman Who Replaced Jane Pauley's Replacement," *The New York Times,* April 8, 1991

Page 53, line 7: Schwarzbaum. "Katie Did It"

Page 54, line 7: Marin, Rick. "He Was Everything I Look For," *Newsweek,* July 6, 1998

Page 54, line 18: Weber, Bruce. "At Home with Katie Couric," *The New York Times,* April 9, 1992

Page 55, line 8: Schwarzbaum, Lisa. "Katie's Couric's Charm Sparks Today Comeback," *Richmond Times-Dispatch.* July 30, 1992

Page 56, line 1: Klein. *Katie: the Real Story*, p. 75

Page 56, line 7: Ibid., p. 76

Page 57, line 2: "Katie Couric," *People*, December 28, 1992

Page 57, line 10: Kaufman, Joanne. "Katie Couric Today," *TV Guide.* February 6, 1993

Page 58, line 11: Klein. *Katie: the Real Story*, p. 85

Page 61, sidebar: Paprocki, Sherry Beck. *Katie Couric.* Penn.: Chelsea House Publishers, 2001, p. 56

Chapter Seven

Page 66, line 5: http://www.pbs.org/newshour/shields&gigot/july96/wrap_7-5.html

Page 66, line 12: Ibid.

Page 66, line 23: DePaulo, Lisa. "Killer Katie," *George*, May 1997

Page 71, line 6: Weber, "At Home with Katie Couric"

Chapter Eight

Page 73, line 5: Marin, "The Katie Factor"

Page 74, line 7: Spector, Rosanne. "A Conversation with Katie Couric: Standing Up for Cancer Research," *Stanford Medicine,* Summer 2008

Page 76, line 10: Powell, Joanna. "Katie's Crusade," *Good Housekeeping,* October 1, 1998

Page 77, line 17: Marin. "He Was Everything I Look For"

Page 77, line 24: June 1998 Avon Women of Enterprise Awards

Page 78, line 5: Marin, "The Katie Factor"

Page 79, sidebar: Perry, Patrick. "Katie Couric confronts colon cancer," *Saturday Evening Post,* January 1, 2004

Page 80, line 15: Klein. *Katie: the Real Story*, p. 117

Page 80, line 20: Marin. "He Was Everything I Look For"

Page 81, line 13: http://www.experiencefestival.com/a/Katie_Couric_-_Personal_life/id/1547192

Page 85, line 14: http://www.msnbc.msn.com/id/12137229

Chapter Nine

Page 87, line 4: Klein. *Katie: the Real Story*, p. 212

Page 88, line 9: Boedeker, Hal. "Katie looks to tomorrow," *Orlando Sentinel,* May 31, 2006

Page 89, line 17: Ibid.

Page 90, line 13: Klein. *Katie: the Real Story*, p. 224

Page 90, line 25: Shister, Gail. "Ratings for 'CBS Evening News' jump with Couric at the helm," *Philadelphia Inquirer*, September 11, 2006

Page 91, line 4: Clehane, Diane. "Woman of the year: 'Couric Effect' brings a human dimension to CBS Evening News," *Daily Variety,* July 28, 2006

INDEX

ABOUT THE AUTHOR

 Rachel A. Koestler-Grack has worked with nonfiction books as an editor and a writer since 1999. She has worked extensively with historical topics, ranging from the Middle Ages to the Colonial Era to the civil rights movement. She has written numerous biographies on a variety of historical and contemporary figures. Rachel lives with her husband and daughter in the German community of New Ulm, Minnesota.

PICTURE CREDITS